Reasons for Smile

Journey of smile from dreams to reality

Reasons for Smile

AARTI MITTAL

Worldwide Published by
Pendown Press

PENDOWN PRESS

An ISO 9001 & ISO 14001 Certified Co.,
Regd. Office: 2525/193, 1st Floor, Onkar Nagar-A,
Tri Nagar, Delhi-110035
Ph.: 09350849407, 09312235086
E-mail: info@pendownpress.com
Branch Office: 1A/2A, 20, Hari Sadan, Ansari Road,
Daryaganj, New Delhi-110002
Ph.: 011-45794768
Website: PendownPress.com

First Edition: 2021

ISBN: 978-93-90116-54-6

Cover, Layout and Illustrations by Pendown Graphics Team
Printed and Bound in India by Thomson Press India Ltd.

Index

Dedication

I am dedicating this book to all family and
friends who were always there to understand
me and gave me their full support in making it
possible for my dream to come true.

Acknowledgements

First and foremost, I would like to thank God for making it possible for the dream in my eyes to become fruitful in the form of his blessings which gave me the courage to start my book.

Friends and Family were and are also there with me.

I am really very thankful to Dinesh Verma, Ceo Pendown Press and his team for their support and suggestions during the creative process.

Last but not least, I would like to thank my lovely kids and wonderful husband for being a constant source of encouragement.

Thank you.

-Aarti-

Request

God request you for a little time,
Please give me that little time.

Dreams had nurtured right now,
Why you want to break them now?

Why you want to snatch my smile from me?
Why you want dreams of mine to be
away from me?

Don't I have any right to fulfil my any dream?
Don't I have any authority to taste life' scream?

If asking this much from you,
what wrong am I doing?
I just need some time to prove myself,
that's all what I am saying.

"U" know very well, they are the ones who had
raised questions on my capability.
I just want to show and prove to them,
what all I have and possess the ability.

They think that they are powerful by binding me
in chains,
They don't know that it is very rare to have
sunshine while it rains.

If ever they give me the opportunity,
I would let them know about my inner unity.

What all I have is of my own, I have nothing of
them,
They only had money, pride and ego and I didn't
want to have anyone of them.

Can't you listen my prayers this time?
Can't you give me a single chance this time?

I don't want to loose this battle,
If lost this, many others will loose this battle.

I am prayers with a pure heart,
I am asking this for my heart.

You know I have to smile forever as promised to
do that,
But they all will not smile if you did all like that.

This time, begging for everyone's smile,
hidden behind their smile is my own smile.

You only said that you want me to be happy,
without proving myself how I can be happy?

Every moment I feel insulted because "u" haven't
given the chance to win.

Want to know this time what was my crime and
what I did the sin?

Request

My crime and my sin if I did
should be paid my me if I did.

No one else should pay for all these,
No one else should cry for all these.

But since I haven't done anything wrong,
why are you punishing me like this?

When I haven't hurt anyone, why are you
blaming me like this?

God blessed me with a kiss on my forehead,
With blessings for bright future on my forehead.

All pains and sorrows left its phase,
Happiness arrived to me in a new face.

Colours, rhymes, songs and fragrances,
Came to me and had changed all tenses.

What was my past I didn't remember, what will
the future, don't want to know,
What is present is what is important to me and
that is all enough for me to know.

Flowers smile with a single sigh of me,
Air blows very soothingly high for me.

Feelings surround me with their emotions,
Nature kisses me with it's quiet motions.

All complaints from life has been lost,
they had paid approvals as it's cost.

God was with me like my own reflection,
waiting for right time for his right action.

He had decided to give all stars to sky,
He wants me to say they all are my.

Moonlight covers to me now to enhance my
beauty,
I asked them why she is doing that, she said its
her duty.

-Aarti-

Life?

Life is a story of beautiful trends,
No one knows from where it starts and where it
ends.

Life is like a song of joy and sorrow.
It is not like lend and borrow.

Life is game,
Where Victory earns a good fame.

Like is like a test,
Where everyone tries his best,

Life is like a flower, Which gives us very sweet
fragrance,
It's like sweet memories entrance.

Life is like a Book,
Which may contain what we want to cook.

Life is like a river having two different shores,
You can name them as sadness & happiness,
A good diver never drowns,
Who crosses the river wins life's crown.

Life is like a dream,
Which may be sour like salt or may be sweet like
Icecream.

Life is not too easy nor too hard,
It's really very difficult to part.

Life is a struggle,

A struggle between thoughts of us,
Reward is happiness given to us.

Life is to Love, and to love is life.

-Aarti-

Life

When you choose me, shown me how life could
be. Given me wings to fly, Makes me feel that
I have a life!

During all that time, Sorrow was to mine.
Colours came to me, as it was Butter fly!
Yes, I have a life!

When you come to me, Air kisses me. All
worries die, yes! You are life.

Show me how life could be…

…I have a life!

Money material is strong enough, Might take
you got you up.

But I am so glad that I have got you. Once I had
been through hard enough, Things were high
that paid Me-Up.

Going through harder…
That has threatened to the luck,

But I know I got it through.
I am so glad that I got you.

Crops were singing, Takes me up,
Sun was blooming, moon said what's-up.

Butterfly comes with its colours,
Find the Ocean so blue.

Yes! Yes! Yes! Darling {Life} it was you,
I am so glad that I have got you.

Smile! Smile! Smile! Not so tough.
My love spreads all around you.

Now I am shocked how I got you!

-Aarti-

Angel

There is a strange feeling in my heart.

Don't know what my heart is trying to say,
whether it is saying to go or asking me to stay.

Everything is here and there, But no one knows
God is where.

Everyone says it is everywhere, You can even feel
him in the air.

Today air is not soothing to me,
It is pinching this time to me.

Tears want to roll down from eyes,
But heart wants them to stay in eyes.

Oh! Dear Angel in the sky Are 'u' listening to
me,

If yes, lend your wings and magic stick to me.

I just want to fly high in sky,
And to shower smiles for everyone
from that high.

Can you do this favour to me?
Can you give all this to me?

It is a wish for happiness of everyone
I just want smiles for everyone.
If you can't give me your stick please do this for
me,
Please give everyone a smile, please do this to me.

-Aarti-

Smile

Smile, Smile, Smile where is this smile?
Give this to me forever not for a while.

Life is to smile and smile is to live,
what will be a better gift to give?

Innocence in your eyes and honesty on your face,
Makes everyone's life going on a nice phase.

You look beautiful with a smile,
And you kill me by your sweet and simple smile.

When your hair blow across your face,
They just make one flattered upon you by just a
stare on your face.

When light flashes upon your eye,
It makes everyone to touch sky and fly.

Your inner beauty is more attractive
than the outer one,
but both effect the people of different one.

Your inner beauty has made me feel proud,
That is a part of matter, which distinguishes you
from rest of the crowd.

You are as pure as a soul can be,
You are as fresh as flowers can be.

You have each colour of life,
You spread fragrances of friendship
in everyone's life.

-Aarti-

God!

I am feeling you, yes I am feeling you,
want to know where am I feeling you?

I am feeling you in the air.

I am feeling you everywhere.

I am with you and you are with me,
this is all what anyone can see.

They can only see but can't feel,
watching doesn't matter, what matters is what
one can feel.

Feeling your smile, killing me while what
I know that is your style.

You are in me and I am in you,
that's all what I want to say to you.

-Aarti-

Wish

There is a strange feeling in my heart.

Don't know what heart is trying to say,
whether it is saying go or asking me to stay.

Everything is here and there,
but no one knows 'God' is where?

Everyone says it is everywhere.
You can even feel him in the air.

Today air is not soothing to me,
It is pinching this time to me,

Tears want to roll down from eyes,
But heart wants them to stay in eyes.

Oh! Dear angel in the sky,
Are 'you' watering to me?
If yes, lend your wings and magic stick to me,
I just want to fly high is sky,
and to shower smiles for everyone from that
high.

Can you do this favour to me?
Can you give all this to me?

It is a wish for happiness of everyone,
I just want smiles for everyone.

If can't give me your stick,
please give everyone a smile,
please do this to me.

-Aarti-

Stage of Life

Different stages of each and everyone's life,
welcoming everything with a sweet smile.

It is not a task which is too easy,
But a work which keeps everyone busy.

Every phase is having it's own importance,
Life is pouring now it's own importance.

Everyone's smile is now desired,
Everyone's happiness is now required.

Now I come to know that what is the value of
my own smile, My smile is important face,
if not for someone It is their life.

A single tear cannot be tolerated,
A mark of sorrow on my face is now being hated.

Always a big smile is being demanded,
All the happiness is being supplied.

A mere statement is taken as a wish,
There is a try and wish to fulfill that wish.

They say that I am source of inspiration to them,
But I don't know what to say to them,

They are not only my inspiration but my smile
too,
Moreover not only smile, but my life too.

-Aarti-

Right are Wrong

Feeling nice are feeling bad,
Feeling gloomy are feeling sad.

Whatever the reasons are, I have to struggle,
whatever the reasons are, I have to fight.

Fed up of each and every time fighting with
myself,
shed up all the curtains of my inner self.

I am on the stage as I am Yes, this is what all I a.,
If mistake is done by me,
then punishment will be honored by me.

But if smile is given by me,
never the credit will be taken by me.

To give counter to yourself everytime, needs
bucket full's of courage,
to punish yourself is courageous, when light is on
your own rage.

I am not a Majesty, because what I did was not a
mere "ere" but a crime.

To punish myself for that, is not only necessary,
but right now my motto which is prime.

Never ever given a single thought to hurt
someone like that, but this is the desired
punishment for that.

-Aarti-

Life

What is all life about?
What is there about here to shout?

No one knows about its existence,
She is the one with all her resistance.

Life with simple and sweet smile,
Life with a beautiful and daring style.

Motto of life to make others smile,
that should be forever and not for a while.

Life looks now like beautiful landscape,
All sorrows and disappointment,
just want to escape.

Answer why life has become like this?
Answer why smile has becomes
o sweet like this?

So many questions but with a single answer,
"It is just because of everyone who is near to me
and who cares about my smile."
It is the only and desired answer.

-Aarti-

Passion

Passion running in veins,
May be clouds forming heavy rains.

Goal set by my soul,
want that I should walk till that goal.

It is known that there are many hurdles in
between,
All the results and consequences are also seen.

Can't quit from the war,
Though goals are still far.

Distances can't let me change my track, Removing
all hurdles one should follow one's track.

Now, when standing on the stairs dream,
It is not tolerable if, I don't get the cream.

One defeat can't let me down,
I am meant to honour the crown.

-Aarti-

Shadow

My own shadow suddenly striked me up,
She very siftly asked 'sweetie' whats' up?

I was shocked to counter my own reflection,
She was just trying to copy my every action.

I offered her my hand for hand shake,
She was not ready to do hand shake.

She suddenly burred down and welcomed me to
her room,
She was so sweet and so as was her room.

She was looking like as sweet angel,
with her hairs well set up with a gel.

She was beautiful with her very sweet smile,
Saying me feeling your smile reeling me while,

In her room there were thousands of Hewers,
Blowing air was throwing them on me with
Shower.

Sunshine with all shine is mine,
Either it is eight or it is nine.

Cupid trying to make me his target,
Filling the atmosphere with love as target.

She presented me with a bunch of flowers,
said me that I am a smile for flower.

I realized it is important for me, as I am
important for my reflection,
Because somewhere it is true that we are each
other's reflection.

-Aarti-

Little Angel

When I closed my eyes I found myself in the
world of fantasy, there was lots of fog around me
and nothing else I can see.

A little angel with a magic stick in her hand,
Asked me to wake up and to stand.

She wiped off my tears and asked me to smile,

Blessing me and moving her stick on me for
smile.

She called up other angels and asked them to
sing a song,
She was doing all this to make right, what all had
went wrong.

She made me stand to dance and sing,
Gifted me a very beautiful ring.

Life with me and with all lights and colours of
hers,
Giving me whatever was hers,
Suddenly everything was so clear,
Fog was removed suddenly dear.

I started feeling all the happiness and colours,
that small angel started filling all colours.

Taking away me from the sorrows and fears,
Made me felt that everyone do cares.

A Bunch of flowers in her hand for me,
A kiss on forehead as a blessing for me.

Hugging me and giving warmth of friendship
Taking me in joy's and smile's ship?

-Aarti-

Challenges

Word ability, capability the things to prove your
sensibility.

The life with lots of challenges and wars to won,
They can be huge in number that can be tone.

Hurdles in the way with all their forces,
Aim is the only thing which the life focuses.

Accepted the challenges and ready to fight,
Knowing without what is wrong and what is right?

Consequences cannot make my goals away from me,
The life is the life whether it is you or me.

Focus of life cannot be shifted,
Aim of file cannot be shifted.

Fire and Passion running and burning in veins,
Inner fight is occurring in the brain.

-Aarti-

Happy New Year!

Music, love, colour, beauty in her arms, Marching
towards is with all her charms.

Leaving behind sorrow & fears,
Bringing for all of us sweet and simple cheers.

Innocently and sweetness shut in her eyes,
That's what makes her everyone choice.

Everyone seems to be flattered on her simplicity
creating a big puzzle that too with a lots of
complexity.

Everyone falling in love with her still her identity
is unknown,
with her eyes as deep as take and as pure as soul
trying to make herself known.

Let secret be secret till the night arrives,
And the clock on the 31st Dec. strikes 12 in mid
might and surprise arrives.

Now, when the designated night is to come
about,
Nature here is to make her arrival known is about
o shout.

With crown of moon on her head,
Showering moon light from these ahead.

Spreading love and colours with there best
combination,
Playing music with each 'n' everyone's heart as
destination.

Passing the blessings of almighty 'gos' to all of us,
Praying for all the happiness of all of us.

Happy New year!

-Aarti-

Destination

A girl in this world with the simple life,
A string in hand of flying rite.

It is in her hand to decide the kite & direction,
It is she only who can fill this with her
imagination.

She with her pretty eyes,
passing her target lens sighs.

Aim some broken some in her hands,
Want to know where exactly she stands.

Darkness speeded all over in the groom,
want to make each other bloom.

Life is to smile and smile is to live.
What is life, it is to gain or to give.

-Aarti-

Friends

Friends are Like, Friends are God,
They are always new for me Will never become
old.

They had given me courage to stand in world,
And made me intelligent and so bold,
That now I can bear also Australia's cold.

If God gives me choice between gold and
friends,
I will not prefer gold but will prefer my friends.

They had changed my life style,
And teached me to live with a smile.

They are those who had filled my life with
happiness and joy,
They are among those who had treated me as a
human not as a toy.

They had teached me to fight for freedom,
But they will rule over always on my heart's
kingdom.

They are as pure as diamond.

I have equal faith on them and God.

They are my Rod, which had shown me right
path.

Thanks God for giving such nice friends, who
care for me, I care for them the thing I know is
that I cheer only for them.

If they are always is my life, I will never be upset,
whether it is sunrise or sunset.

More than diamonds I value my friends.
I wish that our love, friendship never ends.

My life is for them, my smile is for them,
If I am a tree, they are my stem.

-Aarti-

Glamour

You can't see me because I am hidden in a shell,
But you can feel me because I am in the air,

Having my own way to move and many to
follow,
Having my own path to grow.

Might be I am little bit momentary,
But it doesn't mean that I am complementary.

I give pleasure which lasts till the end moment,
Everyone is having my passion whether it is a
teacher or a student.

I am having contemporary life style,
Everyone welcomes me with a 1000 million
smile.

What I mean is to admire a beauty.
Tell me oh! Dear don't you want to be called as
cutie!

Take with me, walk with me,
you will not found anyone sweeter than me.

May be eager to know about me.

-Aarti-

Who Am I? Guess? Ok here I am

G	Gorgeous
L	Loveable
A	Adorable
M	Marvelous
O	Ocarina
U	Ubiquitous
R	Romantic

Which when complied together will sound as.

-Aarti-

Power in Yourself

Power in yourself

Why life seems to be questions to me?
It suddenly brought answer to me.

With lots of cuddles, with lots of joy,
with lots of things to play but not with a toy.

Moving with a ray of hope hiding in a deep
corner of your heart.

Moving things around but that's not in a flowers
most.

Not to take a back step untill you get what you
want,

Keeping a prayer deep in your heart with lots of
chant.

If your soul is pure and your will is true,

All success is in your hand and you will get them
through.

-Aarti-

Unclear Picture of Life

Don't know from where this life begins and
where it ends,
I don't know even the life trends.

Hiding my emotions, or killing them,
I am repeating the leaves from stem.

The dreams with whom I was walking,
I had nobody with myself for talking.

God on every step was taking my test,
I without giving myself no rest.

Why I am not satisfied with every my ability,
why things don't move according to my
suitability.

Everything's seems behind dark clouds to me,
It is very difficult to see even the things which
are near to me.

Tears want to roll down from these eyes,
I can't hide them, I am not that much clever nor
that much wise.

Emotions shut down in this stupid heart,
How can I mark the things I do not like on the
chart.

No one realises the things which hurt me slowly
and deeply, why everything is hurting me.

Why I am like this, why things are like this to
me, Why everything is not clear to me.

-Aarti-